The Little Book
of Secrets

**81 Secrets for enjoying a happy, prosperous, and
successful life**

By Chris Prentiss

POWER PRESS, LOS ANGELES

The Little Book of Secrets

81 secrets for living a happy, prosperous and successful life

By Chris Prentiss

Power Press, 1310 Riviera Avenue, Venice, CA 90291.
Telephone: (310) 392-9393 Fax: (310) 392-7710.
Email: chrisprentiss@power-press.com

Library of Congress Card Number: 99-75052

ISBN: 0-943015-33-2

Copyright © 2000 Chris Prentiss Family Trust

First Edition

10 9 8 7 6 5 4 3 2

Author's Apology
To Women Readers

I sincerely apologize for using *he, his, him* when speaking generally. Using *he/she* throughout becomes cumbersome for the reader and disturbs the flow of thought. I chose to use the masculine form because it is what we are accustomed to seeing in print and because the goal is to make the reading easy.

Author's Affirmation

I affirm that the secrets in this book are real secrets that have withstood not just the test of centuries, but of millennia; thousands of years. Knowing these secrets, we can avoid the pitfalls that beset the path of the unenlightened, and soar upward to the heights of success and great good fortune. By taking them to heart and treasuring them, they will bring us riches and benefits beyond anything we currently believe possible. The 81 secrets form a path that leads to having what we desire. Following that path creates a river of joy within us. I wish you a wonder-filled journey.

-Chris

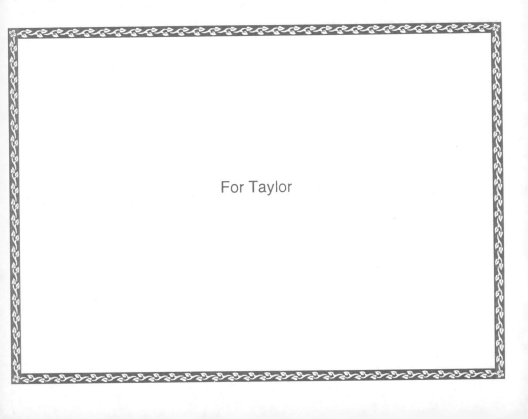

For Taylor

Secret #1

*Exceptional enterprises cannot succeed
unless the utmost caution is observed
in their beginnings.
A situation only becomes favorable
when one adapts to it.*

About the secret

In the beginning of even small things, exceptional care must be exercised if a planting is to lead to a flowering. How much more then should exceptional care be exercised when great or dangerous undertakings are begun? A flaw, built into the beginning, increases with time, and, if not corrected, will ultimately cause the failure of the enterprise. The knowledgeable, successful person can always see the end in the beginning; he knows the seeds and, exercising great care, enjoys a lifetime of success and good fortune.

Secret #2

*By manifesting a modest attitude,
people will naturally want to help us
and give us good counsel.*

About the secret

It is a part of human nature to love and help the modest and to resent and thwart the arrogant. People soon give up helping or counseling an egotistical person who thinks he knows everything. When we are modest, people do not resent us, and consequently, we do not incur opposition. The attainment of our goals becomes easy, and we readily attract helpers. Because we like to tell others of our accomplishments and of our talents, it is sometimes difficult to be modest, but the rewards of modesty are far greater than the pleasures of telling of our accomplishments and talents. Practicing this one secret will do more for our success than five years of hard work, and our success will soar as high as the great redwood trees.

Secret #3

Do not hate.
Hatred binds us to the hated object.

About the secret

The Universe is favorably inclined. That is how and why it continues. That means that there is more goodness than evilness. Hatred is a product of evil. To the extent we allow ourselves to feel hatred, to that extent we become an instrument of evil. When we hate someone, our strong emotion draws that person to us. Is that what we want? To eliminate the connection, we simply dismiss the person from our thoughts. To combat evil, we respond with goodness. Evil cannot exist where goodness thrives.

Secret #4

Take not gain or loss to heart.
What man holds high
comes to nothing.

About the secret

We are not our gain; neither are we our loss. Gains and losses are external to us, things with which our eternal soul is not concerned. All gains and losses pass away at the time of death. Do not waste even a moment on gains and losses when death is plucking our ears saying, "Live! I am coming."

Secret #5

*In general,
opposition appears as an obstruction,
but the knowledgeable person
uses it to his advantage.*

About the secret

Upon encountering opposition, the inferior person, ignorant of the laws of the Universe, bewails his fate, blames others or circumstances, and quits his efforts. The wise person, knowledgeable in the laws of the Universe, uses the opposition to gather strength, improve himself, and take a more beneficial course of action. He sees the opposition as an opportunity and seeks the cause of the opposition within himself, and through this introspection, the external opposition becomes, for him, an occasion of inner enrichment and education. Adversity is for our strengthening. A person of true understanding takes each ounce of adversity and turns it to his advantage. By adopting this attitude regarding opposition, our strength will grow as a young bear's, and we will reach our goals as though on the back of Pegasus himself, the fabled winged horse.

Secret #6

*Passion and reason
cannot exist side by side.*

About the secret

When anger, lust, hatred, or love consumes us, clear, rational thinking is impossible. It is only when we are able to calmly step back from ourselves and "look in on ourselves" that true detachment is achieved, which then permits rational thinking. When we achieve that goal, we make no mistakes.

Secret #7

*In times of prosperity
it is important
to possess enough greatness of spirit
to bear with the mistakes of others.*

About the secret

Just as water washes everything clean, the wisest person pardons mistakes and even forgives intentional transgressions. In that way he insures the upward spiral of his prosperity. The inferior person cannot resist the opportunity to chastise another and, in so doing, brings resentment onto himself, destroys unanimity, and crushes enthusiasm, thereby destroying his own chances for success. When our star is on the rise, we need only keep our eyes fixed upon it, forgiving all mistakes and transgressions, and we will be drawn to the heights of success as a kite in a strong wind.

Secret #8

*When entangled in a conflict
it is wise
to remain so clear headed and strong
that we are always ready
to come to terms with our opponent
by meeting him halfway.*

About the secret

In times of conflict we are always in danger because our opponent is seeking to harm us. Taking an opportunity to end the conflict by meeting our opponent half-way leads away from a time of danger to a time of security. That is a wise and sensible course of action, and the knowledgeable, successful person seizes the opportunity, knowing that, in truth, he has won a great victory. To carry on a conflict to the bitter end has evil effects because, even if we win, the enmity is then continued.

Secret #9

*If we want to know what anyone is like,
we have only to observe
on what he bestows his care
and what sides of his own nature
he cultivates and nourishes.*

About the secret

Each person reveals himself by what he says and does, by the way he dresses, by the ways he responds to events, by what he reads and watches, by the way he stands, by the way he is regarded by his friends and associates, and generally, by the way he lives life. By observing anyone, we can see what that person is like.

Secret #10

Boasting of
power, wealth, position, promotion,
success, or influential friends
inevitably
invites misfortune and humiliation.

About the secret

Boasting only confirms that we feel inferior, inadequate, and insecure and that we are trying to add to our stature by our boasting. It also displays a great lack of understanding of human nature, which universally dislikes a braggart. The knowledgeable person considers what he has sufficient and lets it speak for itself. He acts modestly, and in that way assures his continued success, for the world loves a modest person.

Secret #11

*The way of the happy, successful person
is to be joyous of heart,
yet concerned in thought.*

About the secret

The happy, successful person is concerned in thought because he knows that all periods of prosperity are followed by times of decline and all people are not as they should be. He therefore takes thought for the future and exercises caution in his dealings with people. Nonetheless, no matter how concerned he is in thought, nor how weighty those thoughts may be, his concerns are never enough to dim his inner joy because, above all, he remains aware that he is an indestructible child of a golden Universe.

Secret #12

To a person of true understanding
it makes no difference
whether death comes early or late.

About the secret

We may have forgotten how we got here, but we do know the way because we are alive at this moment. When we come to know that we are the Universe, a part of it, as much as the stars and the mountains and the planets, and that, as the Universe is eternal, we are eternal, we use whatever time we have while we're here to cultivate ourselves and use the time productively. Our sense of the transitoriness of life does not impel us to uninhibited revelry in order to enjoy life while it lasts, nor to yield to melancholy and sadness, thereby spoiling the time remaining to us. Knowing that time is only an illusion, we feel no break with time. Understanding this, we need have no fear of the moment of death, which is only a point of transition, such as walking through a doorway from one room into another and no more remarkable than any other moment.

Secret #13

*For power to be truly great
it must remain inwardly united
with the fundamental principles
of right and justice.*

About the secret

The inferior person, concerned only for his own well being and pleasure, uses his power to further his own selfish ends and to cause hurt and trouble for others. This is degenerative use of power and bodes ill for everyone, particularly the wielder of the power. The knowledgeable person, concerned with the principles of right and justice, uses his power to aid others and improve the general welfare. This bodes well for everyone, particularly the wielder of the power.

Secret #14

*When we see good,
we should imitate it.
If we have faults,
we should rid ourselves of them.*

About the secret

Those are two of the most favorable character attributes we can cultivate; they lead to great good fortune and success. It is one of the ways the knowledgeable, successful person further brightens his already bright virtue. For persevering in that effort, even among those considered lucky we will stand out as the chosen ones.

Secret #15

*In the hands of a great master,
everything and everyone is useful.*

About the secret

A great master can find a use for everything and everyone, and he is good at salvage. He wastes nothing; therefore, he always has enough. He values everyone; therefore, everyone values him.

Secret #16

*Pleasant manners succeed
even with irritable people.*

About the secret

If we do not allow the irritability of others
to affect our own pleasant conduct, our
pleasant conduct then influences them.
For prevailing in this secret, our friends
and associates will grow as sunflowers
after a warm summer rain.

Secret #17

*It is wise and reasonable
not to try to obtain anything
by force.*

About the secret

That which is obtained by force must be held by force. That constant exertion drains our energy, invites the censure of others, and inevitably leads to regret. It is a law of the Universe that what we obtain by force will ultimately bring us misfortune in one form or another, and a knowledgeable, successful person will have none of it. While it may appear that something obtained by force is a temporary benefit to the person who obtained it, in the end, the law will be fulfilled.

Secret #18

*Conflict within
weakens the power to conquer
danger without.*

About the secret

When the time for action has come, conflict within us causes us to hesitate. Conflict within a group will prevent members of the group from acting as a unit. In either case, conflict weakens. Great or dangerous undertakings are to be avoided in times of conflict because achieving success requires a concerted unity of force. Making certain that there is no inner conflict when the time for action is at hand will find us ever victorious.

Secret #19

*The small-minded person
is not ashamed of unkindness
and does not shrink from injustice.*

About the secret

The inferior person is unconcerned with unfairness or unkindness. As a result of natural law, he suffers, and he does not know that he is the cause of his suffering. The successful person feels diminished by acts of unkindness or injustice, whether committed by himself or another. As a result of natural law, he enjoys a life of great good fortune and contentment. He is highly regarded by his friends and close associates, and he easily walks the path that leads to success, looked up to by all.

Secret #20

*It is better to go on foot
than ride in a carriage
under false pretenses.*

About the secret

It is better to go honorably on foot and do without than to ride in a fine carriage under false pretenses and thereby lose our honor. If we pretend abundance when in fact we are in need, those who would aid us will not, either by believing us to be abundant or by recognizing our pretense and considering us to be unworthy. Furthermore, by pretending we have something when we do not, we diminish ourselves in our own eyes and so lose self-respect. It is "who we think we are" that we are.

Secret #21

*To be a knowledgeable, successful person,
we should acquaint ourselves with many sayings of antiquity
and many deeds of the past,
and thus strengthen our characters.*

About the secret

A strong character is what determines all our actions and thoughts. Our actions and thoughts determines our future. By studying the sayings that have survived the test of the centuries, we gain wisdom. By learning of the deeds of our ancient heroes, we gain inspiration. Wisdom, coupled with inspiration, leads to great good fortune and supreme success.

Secret #22

*Once we have gained
inner mastery of a problem,
it will come about naturally
that the action we take
will succeed.*

About the secret

Gaining inner mastery of a problem begins with our recognition that the problem is in our lives because it holds a gift for us; it presents us with an opportunity for improving ourselves or our situation. Thinking our way through the problem, keeping in mind that the solution will put us in better circumstances than before the problem arose, or that it will prevent us from making an error, will result in the success of any action we take. Anyone who masters that secret will rise high and reach every state that mortals can desire.

Secret #23

To be a knowledgeable, successful person,
see to it
that goodness
is an established attribute of character
rather than
an accidental and isolated occurrence.

About the secret

True goodness means that our intentions are always beneficial, never hurtful. To maintain our beneficial intentions, it is necessary to renew our determination every day to follow the path of the knowledgeable, successful person, always working to improve our character. For persevering in our efforts, we will find within ourselves a wellspring of joy that will refresh and renew us all of our days, and good fortune and success will follow as closely as do our shadows in the full light of the sun.

Secret #24

In cultivating oneself,
it is best to root out bad habits
and tolerate those that are harmless.

About the secret

If we are too weak to overcome habits that are obviously bad for us, our future is indeed bleak. While temporary pleasures may accompany bad habits, they are, in the long run, detrimental to us and, even in the short run, weaken us. Acquiring a long-run problem in exchange for a short-run pleasure is a poor bargain. It takes strength and determination to rid ourselves of bad habits that control us, but by so doing, we gain control, increase our strength, and have a supremely better life. A knowledgeable, successful person is always in control of his habits. To be successful in rooting out bad habits, it is, however, wise to tolerate less harmful habits for a time, for if we are too strict with ourselves, we may fail in our purpose.

Secret #25

To act on the spur of every whim,
ultimately
leads to humiliation.

About the secret

What the heart desires, we run after without a moment's hesitation, but there are three restraints that ought to be given consideration: first, we should not run after all persons we would like to influence, but should hold back if it seems improper for us to make an approach; second, we should not yield to every whim of those in whose service we are; third, where the moods of the heart are concerned, we should not ignore the possibility of holding back, for this is the basis of human freedom. Develop the strength to choose a wise course of action even in the face of desires that pull us in a different direction. This is very difficult, but essential if we are to be in charge of our fate, and leads to great success and supreme good fortune.

Secret #26

*To enjoy a meaningful way of life,
and to produce long-lasting effects,
the ability to endure
must be firmly established
within us.*

About the secret

To endure means to continue in the face of obstacles, pain, fatigue, frustration, opposition, or hardship. To endure is to continue to the end. Duration is a state that is not worn down by anything. It seems almost needless to say that when we have established the quality of endurance within ourselves, we can reach any goal, overcome any obstacle, and bear any condition. Once established, that inner law of our being then determines all of our actions and leads to extraordinary good fortune and abundant success. Gaining mastery of that one secret, allows us to completely depend upon ourselves to persevere until our goals are reached.

Secret #27

*To be successful,
we should not be rigid and immobile
in our thinking,
but always keep abreast of the time
and
change with it.*

About the secret

The universal law that provides for constant change is the only thing that does not change. To remain inflexible when all else is changing is to invite disaster. It is essential to our success that we set a firm course and that we be stable enough in our character not to waver with every passing fad; it is equally essential, however, that we be aware of changing conditions and be open and flexible enough in our thinking to change with changing conditions. Maintaining rigidity leads to failure; remaining flexible leads to success.

Secret #28

If we attempt too much,
we will end
by succeeding
in nothing.

About the secret

It is commendable to push ourselves to new heights; we can thereby increase our strength and reach ever greater success. If, however, we strive to reach unrealistic or unattainable goals, we court disaster and failure and may lose even that which we already have. The knowledgeable, successful person does not overreach himself, overspend himself, or strive foolishly. In that way he enjoys a lifetime of success.

Secret #29

*To remain at the mercy
of moods
of hope and fear
will cost us
our inner composure and consistency.*

About the secret

Hope contains the subtle fear that what we hope for will not come to pass. Fear contains the subtle hope that what we fear will not come to pass. Neither state is appropriate to the knowledgeable, successful person who turns everything to his advantage, and who therefore knows that everything that occurs is for his benefit. To remain at the mercy of hope and fear is to bob like a cork on the ocean, rising and falling as our hopes and fears assail us. Living the life of the knowledgeable, successful person is certain to secure our fate and bring us supreme success and good fortune. Therefore, we must have courage and faith, and be joyous, and all will be well. We are far more powerful than we suspect, and the universal plan includes our well being.

Secret #30

*If we live in a state of perpetual hurry,
we will fail to attain inner composure.*

About the secret

Inner composure means having a settled state of mind; calmness, tranquillity. Whoever attains that state is then able to act without stress and therefore makes no mistakes. Constant hurrying wears us down, destroys our calmness, and puts lines in our faces. By slowing down and nurturing ourselves with the ways of the knowledgeable, successful person, all else will be achieved through the process of natural law.

Secret #31

*When confronted with insurmountable forces
retreat is proper.*

About the secret

If we persist in fighting a battle that is beyond our capabilities, we risk depleting our resources so greatly that we cannot recover. To retreat does not mean to give up. On the contrary, retreating preserves resources and allows us time to regain our strength, renew our forces, and make new plans. Thus, retreat makes possible a counter-movement, which makes possible our success.

Secret #32

*Power
best expresses itself
in gentleness.*

About the secret

The bully, the despot, and the person in authority who uses his power to hurt others are all universally disliked. They create their own unpleasant environment within which they must exist. By contrast, the knowledgeable, successful person in a position of power can be clearly recognized by his gentleness. His gentle expression of power does not provoke resentment nor incur resistance, and so makes easy the attainment of his purposes and the continued growth of his power. By following the example of the knowledgeable, successful person, we will go our way unopposed on a smooth, easy road.

Secret #33

*The knowledgeable person
is never led into baseness
or vulgarity
by community of interests
with people of low character.*

About the secret

We sometimes find ourselves associating with inferior people because of the need to achieve a common goal. In their company we may be tempted to pleasures and actions that are inappropriate for the knowledgeable, successful person. To participate in such low pleasures or actions would certainly bring remorse. Just as we should not allow ourselves to be unresistingly swept along by unfavorable circumstances, neither should we allow inferior people to erode our good character. By our determination to continue in what we know to be right, we will overcome even the greatest of adversities, and success and good fortune will naturally come to us.

Secret #34

*In financial matters,
well being prevails
when expenditures and income
are in proportion.*

About the secret

Out of debt; out of danger. We must not spend more than we have; credit enslaves. Since all periods of prosperity are followed by periods of decline, the knowledgeable, successful person prepares for the times of decline during the times of prosperity. If we always spend all that we have, we will be unprepared in times of emergency. Such poor planning leads to the destruction of well being and invites disaster. Whoever masters this one secret will live a life of such great abundance that, from the excess, he will be able to experience the joy of giving.

Secret #35

There is no need to be ashamed
of
simplicity
or
small means.

About the secret

Simplicity is the hallmark of the knowledgeable, successful person, ostentation, or showing off, the hallmark of the unknowledgeable, unsuccessful person. There is no need to present false appearances; even with slender means, or no means at all, the sentiment of the heart can be expressed. It is not for the price of our gift that we are appreciated, but for the sentiment with which it is given and the value we hold in the eyes of the receiver. And making a show of what we have never endears us to our friends and neighbors.

Secret #36

*A compromise with evil
is not possible.*

About the secret

To end a conflict with evil-minded people, we are sometimes tempted to compromise what we know to be right. Such compromising is an error, for evil must be completely eradicated if it is not to spring up again. The best way to overcome evil is to hold completely to what is good. To digress even slightly from that path is to start on the path of the inferior and unsuccessful person. To continue on that path can only lead to unfortunate results.

Secret #37

In the time of gathering together,
we should make no arbitrary choice of our associates.
There are secret forces at work,
leading together
those who belong together.

About the secret

An arbitrary choice is one that is made on the basis of personal preference, without regard to laws or principles. In the time of gathering together, the secret forces that are leading together those of us who belong together may bring people who are not of our personal preference but who, nonetheless, may be of great benefit to us. The secret, therefore, counsels us in two ways: one, that we should remain open-minded, and two, that we need not concern ourselves about finding the right people.

Secret #38

*We must not allow ourselves
to be led astray
by a leader.*

About the secret

That is not to say we should ignore a leader or good counsel from a qualified person, but that we should question whether a leader's course is best or honorable for us, and then make our own decision about which course to take, always being alert for that little inner voice possessed by each of us that prompts us in the right course of action.

Secret #39

Those things in our psychic bodies
later manifest
in our physical bodies.

About the secret

The mind is a creator, and what we hold there manifests itself in one way or another. If we hold worrying and stress in our minds, they will manifest themselves in our bodies as tension and pain. If we hold thankfulness and joy in our minds, they will manifest themselves in our bodies as radiant health and shining faces. The use of this one secret can magically transform our lives, bringing us great joy, serene lives, and happiness to spare.

Secret #40

*Only when we
go to meet our fate
resolutely
will we be equipped
to deal with it
adequately.*

About the secret

To meet fate resolutely means that we have the determination to overcome whatever fate may bring, that we will not succumb to folly or temptation, and that we will not be turned aside from our chosen course. Only strong and courageous people can stand up to their fate, overcoming all obstacles. Their fierce determination enables them to endure to the end. This strength or courage shows itself in facing things exactly as they are, without any sort of self-deception or illusion. It is then that a light develops out of events by which enables us to recognize the path to success. By making that strong commitment, we actually cause favorable events to occur that would otherwise not have occurred. A person capable of this kind of commitment can reach any goal, overcome any obstacle, and fulfill any plan.

Secret #41

Slander
will be silenced
if
we do not gratify it
with injured retorts.

About the secret

We can spend a lifetime tracking down and defending ourselves against the negative things people say. We should simply go on with our own affairs. With nothing to keep the talk alive, it dies for lack of attention. The best defense against slander is to live the life of the knowledgeable, successful person, letting our actions and conduct speak for us.

Secret #42

*On the road to success,
as we near the attainment of our goal,
we must beware of becoming intoxicated
with our achievement.*

About the secret

If we allow ourselves to become overly excited about an approaching success, we may become careless or light-headed and fail to pay attention to crucial matters and thereby ruin our success. It is precisely at the point of success that we must remain sober and cautious. By maintaining the same attitude and course of action that brought us to the point of success, we will surely and safely achieve our success.

Secret #43

*If we neglect
our good qualities and virtues,
we will cease to be of value
to our friends and neighbors.
Soon,
no one will seek us out
or bother about us.*

About the secret

By nurturing our good qualities and virtues, we insure that our inner worth will be inexhaustible, like a spring of sparkling, clear water and all will seek us out. The more that is drawn from us, the more that remains, and the greater will become our wealth. Those who understand these words will find them more precious than diamonds and gold.

Secret #44

*We can succeed in life,
no matter our circumstances,
provided
we have determination
and endurance,
and follow the path
of the knowledgeable, successful person.*

About the secret

Whatever we now do, whatever we now believe, whatever our current circumstances may be, we are perfectly equipped and fully capable of fulfilling our needs and desires. The opportunities to achieve success are endless, and even those of us who start with nothing can succeed, but even the finest opportunity in the wrong hands comes to nothing. All that is necessary for us to achieve success, great success, is to cultivate endurance as an established trait of character, have determination to reach our goals, and to follow the path of the knowledgeable, successful person. By accomplishing that we will speed to our success as eagles in flight.

Secret #45

*In order to achieve a quiet heart,
rest and movement
must follow each other
in accordance
with the demands of the time.*

About the secret

A quiet heart, meaning a contented, peaceful heart, is among the greatest possessions we can have. Achieving a quiet heart allows us to be sensitive to the subtle promptings from the world around us, which, in turn, allows us to move effortlessly and smoothly through life rather than with great effort and blundering. Acting in accord with the demands of the time produces harmony. If, however, we are still when the time for action comes, we will miss our opportunity, and what would have been easy to achieve becomes difficult. Or, if we are in motion when the time for rest is at hand, we will be unprepared when the time for action comes . The knowledgeable and successful person first achieves a quiet heart, and then acts. Whoever acts from those deep levels makes no mistakes.

Secret #46

*In exercises in meditation
and concentration,
trying to force results
will lead to an unwholesome outcome.*

About the secret

Trying to obtain by force that which can only be obtained by relaxation and calmness will produce results opposite from the ones we hope to achieve. By first achieving inner composure, we can develop meditation and concentration naturally, thereby producing the desired result. Meditation and concentration are valuable tools. Meditation, a quieting of the mind, a cessation of thoughts, allows us to receive input from the subtle levels of the Universe. Concentration, a focusing of our thoughts, permits us to plan successfully. By learning to meditate and concentrate, our successful futures are assured.

Secret #47

*The knowledgeable, successful person
spends a lifetime
developing strong character,
and so
enjoys a lifetime
of supreme good fortune
and great success.*

About the secret

A tree on a mountain develops slowly, according to the law of its being, and consequently stands firmly rooted. So also, the development of one's character must undergo gradual development if it is to have a broad, stable base. The very gradualness of the development makes it necessary, however, to have perseverance lest slow progress become stagnation. For being successful in our efforts, we, also, will enjoy a lifetime of supreme good fortune and great success.

Secret #48

The knowledgeable person
sees
and understands
the transitory, that which is temporary,
in the light of eternity.

About the secret

We imagine an endless future stretching out ahead of us and an endless past stretching out behind. We believe that where we exist is the moment we call "now," the moment we believe to be a tiny hairline that separates the future from the past. The reverse is true; all there is and was and ever will be is an endless "now." Is it not always "now"? The knowledgeable person understands that this moment we call "now" is all that exists and, as such, is as much of eternity as eternity itself. He therefore understands that whatever occurs within this moment of "now," is perfect, just as eternity is perfect. Carrying his thought further, he understands that being part of eternity, he is perfect—and we are perfect. Anyone who completely grasps that concept will feel his sense of impermanence evaporating as mist in the air.

Secret #49

*If
we would have our relationships endure,
we must fix our minds
on an end that endures.*

About the secret

All relationships run the danger that misunderstandings and disagreements will arise that can cause a parting of the ways. If we permit ourselves to drift along without having in mind the fixed goal of the continuation of a relationship, we may find that it continues or not, as the day may determine. By making a commitment to permanently maintain a relationship, we will have set a standard against which all of our actions and decisions affecting the relationship are measured. Having done that, we will avoid the pitfalls and reefs that confront the closer relationships of people. Being successful in this secret, we will be blessed with long lasting friendships and beautiful, rewarding, soul-satisfying relationships.

Secret #50

*Mad pursuit of pleasure
never
takes us to the goal.*

About the secret

No matter what our goals are, if we examine our motives in choosing the goals, we will discover that we have chosen them, one and all, because we believe that they will bring us happiness. Those of us who seek our happiness in the mad pursuit of pleasure experience only temporary sensory enjoyment; we never arrive at our goal of true happiness. Following the path of the knowledgeable, successful person produces happiness, leads to happiness, and maintains happiness; deep down, soul-drenching happiness.

Secret #51

*Waiting
should not be
mere empty hoping;
it should be filled with
the inner certainty
of reaching the goal.*

About the secret

Uncertain of reaching our goals, our waiting will be filled with worrying and fearful imaginings, both of which are detrimental to productivity, and lead away from success. Certain of reaching our goals, our waiting will be filled with happy thoughts and useful occupation, both of which lead directly to success.

Secret #52

*Even with just a
small bit of power,
we can achieve great success
if we use that power correctly.*

About the secret

To use a small bit of power correctly: first, we fix our goal firmly in our minds; seeing it clearly. Then, we imagine ourselves attaining it. Next, we commit ourselves to reaching the goal, and last, we use whatever power we have to always move in the direction of attainment, taking every opportunity that comes along and turning it to our advantage. Our perseverance must never slacken. A key element is that we do not allow opposing thoughts to dwell in our minds. And then, just as dripping water eventually wears away the hardest rock, we will eventually arrive at our goals. To accomplish a great goal with a only a small amount of power is a wonderful accomplishment, bringing us great respect, good fortune and supreme success. Our power will then blossom, and we will accomplish other, greater deeds.

Secret #53

*After a matter
has been thoroughly considered,
it is essential
to form a decision
and
to act.*

About the secret

Reflection or pondering must not be carried too far, lest either cripple the power of decision. When the time for action has come, the moment must be seized. Once a matter has been thoroughly considered, anxious hesitation is a mistake that is bound to bring disaster because we will have missed our opportunity.

Secret #54

*Knowledge
is the key to freedom.*

About the secret

Knowing how to earn a living frees us from poverty. Knowing how to keep healthy frees us from sickness. Knowing how to entertain ourselves frees us from boredom. Knowing the path of the knowledgeable, successful person frees us from misfortune, failure, and suffering.

Secret #55

Through hardness and selfishness,
the heart grows rigid,
and this rigidity
leads to
separation from others.

About the secret

When we see someone in need and turn away from them, that is the beginning of hardness. When someone asks us for help, and we refuse, selfishly hoarding what we have, the hardness grows. When someone asks us for forgiveness, and we refuse, that is the beginning of rigidity. Soon, we begin to look at everyone from behind a mask of hardness. That is our protection against their plea for help. Our voices become sharp, and our manner truculent. Everyone avoids us except the hangers-on who are after the few crumbs that fall from our table. Hardness and selfishness are characteristics of the inferior person. Gentleness and generosity are characteristics of the knowledgeable, successful person. Hardness and selfishness, gentleness and generosity; each bring their own inevitable results.

Secret #56

Unlimited possibilities
are not suited to us.
If they existed,
our lives would only dissolve
into the boundless.

About the secret

Who is it that could choose among unlimited possibilities? Just to consider them would take all of eternity. Limitations are troublesome, but they are effective. The knowledgeable, successful person sets limits within which he experiences total freedom. In so doing, he achieves focus and success and avoids danger. When we come to know the secret of limitation, we will have avoided one of the most dangerous pitfalls to success, and we will rise to dizzying heights of success.

Secret #57

*Through words and deeds
the knowledgeable person
moves
heaven and earth.*

About the secret

By our words and deeds we create good fortune and misfortune. Therefore, shouldn't we be careful of what we say and do? All words and deeds spring from within. If our hearts are pure and our motivations that of the knowledgeable, successful person, our words will be direct and powerful, and our actions will produce far reaching, beneficial effects. If our hearts are not as they should be, can anything else happen but that we fall into a pit of our own creation?

Secret #58

*If we depend on our relationships
for our happiness,
we will either be happy or sad
as our relationships
rise or fall.*

About the secret

That is the fate of those who depend on others for their happiness. To avoid such a fate, we should wed our happiness to that which endures: the path of the knowledgeable, successful person. A quiet, self-contained joy, desiring nothing from without, and resting content with everything, remains independent and free, and in this freedom lies good fortune because it harbors the quiet security of a heart fortified within itself.

Secret #59

*Exceptional
modesty and conscientiousness
are sure to be rewarded
with
great success
and
good
fortune.*

About the secret

Being modest means that we have cultivated a humble attitude and we do not give ourselves airs or strut around trying to impress people; nor are we boastful of our accomplishments. Being conscientious means that we fulfill our tasks and obligations with great care. If we are exceptionally modest and conscientious in a high position, our radiance will be like the sun at mid-day, and no blame or resentment will attach to our progress. The attainment of our goals will be rapid and easy. If we are exceptionally modest and conscientious and hold a low position, we will be recognized and rewarded, and we will rise quickly through the ranks.

Secret #60

*The knowledgeable, successful person
is reverent;
at all times
acknowledging the great creator
and the wonderousness
of the Universe.*

About the secret

When we see a great painting, we acknowledge the painter. When we see a great structure, we acknowledge the builder. When we see the Universe, that tiny portion of it that is visible to us, how can we fail to acknowledge its creator? When great grief or misfortune or illness befalls us, and no human can help, we instinctively turn to the divine for help; that is only natural, since each of us inherently knows the truth of his existence and origin. None of us can fathom how this Universe of ours began, nor can any of us foretell when it will end. Not one of us can even say why it, or we, exist. Since we can only wonder at it all, does it not seem immensely egotistical and foolish not to be reverent in the face of that awesomeness?

Secret #61

*The knowledgeable, successful person
is completely sincere
in his thoughts and actions.*

About the secret

In sorrow and reverence, our feelings must mean more to us than ceremoniousness, which is primarily for the benefit of others. In personal expenditures, we must place the highest value on thrift. In conduct, our actions should be simple and unpretentious. Neither should we pretend love or other emotions that we do not feel; like all false illusions, they only bring hurt and despair in their train and bode ill for the perpetrator. There is no need to pretend or deceive; we need only to fix our eyes on the path of the knowledgeable, successful person, be ourselves, and all else will be accomplished as a result of natural law.

Secret #62

*It is only after
perfect balance
has been achieved
that any misstep
brings imbalance.*

About the secret

It is only after the achievement of success, wealth, fame, happiness, love, popularity, or possessions that we can be burdened with the fear of losing them. This is a caution that we are to remain modest and vigilant once we have acquired our treasure, whatever it is, or the same law that brought it to us will remove it or cause it to work to our detriment. We should not be deluded that our achievements and possessions are the end-all be-all of life. They are merely the objects we have chosen to lead ourselves along the path of life. It is the path itself that is the end-all be-all of life, for on that path we shall learn the lessons of life and perfect ourselves as divine incarnations.

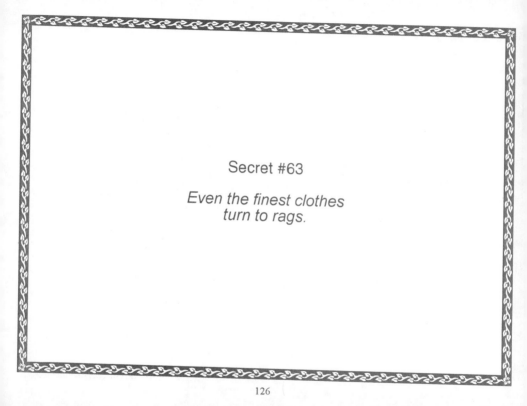

Secret #63

*Even the finest clothes
turn to rags.*

About the secret

Everything, the moment it is made, begins to decay. Is it wise, therefore, to set much store in finery and other such objects? The knowledgeable, successful person does not attach great importance to things that decay. He does attach great importance to those things which endure: his integrity, his honor, his virtue, his appreciation and reverence for All-That-Is. That is not to say that we should not value our possessions, for they bring much pleasure, but that we should not set great store by them, for they are transitory, and there are other, greater treasures.

Secret #64

*There is no plain that is not followed by a slope,
no increase that is not followed by a decrease.*

About the secret

In our constantly changing Universe, the forces of light and dark, good and bad, prosperity and decline, are ever alternating, the increase of one bringing a decrease in the other. It is an eternal law of the Universe that everything, when it reaches its maximum potential, turns toward its opposite. Knowing that law, the knowledgeable, successful person provides for a time of decrease in times of prosperity. He builds himself up during times of good health and so prepares against a time of illness. He takes precautions in times of safety that protect him in times of danger. He thinks ahead and, in so doing, is prepared. He thereby enjoys a lifetime of supreme good fortune and wonderful success.

Secret #65

*We should not complain,
but always enjoy and be grateful for
the good fortune
we still possess.*

About the secret

In an undesirable situation or confronted with a loss, the inferior person bitterly complains and curses his luck. The knowledgeable, successful person remembers the good things still left to him and smiles. He knows that the seemingly undesirable situation or loss will ultimately be a benefit to him; thus, he responds in a positive way. One is sad; one is glad. Each is in charge of his response; each has set the pattern for the continuing course of events. Those of us who master that one secret, will find ourselves always in the best possible situations, enjoying the wonders life holds for the enlightened.

Secret #66

*If
we are not dazzled by enticing goals,
and
remain true to ourselves,
we will travel through life
unassailed,
on a smooth and level road.*

About the secret

Great riches or enticements that dazzle us may also cause us to attempt to get them by means that are inappropriate. Such actions always lead to remorse. If we are true to ourselves, if we live up to the best within us, we will walk the path of the knowledgeable, successful person and, in so doing, will reap the rewards of a prince and the glory of a king.

Secret #67

*At the beginning of a project,
if many boastful claims are made,
the successful attainment of the goal
becomes
far more difficult.*

About the secret

When no claims are put forward, no resistance arises. By cultivating modesty, we will make swift, sure progress because no resentment will attach to us. If we remain modest despite our merit, we will be beloved and will win the support necessary to carry out even difficult and dangerous undertakings. When we make boastful claims, even if we are moderately successful but fall short of our claims, people will say that we failed. Knowing that one secret will make the attainment of our goals far easier.

Secret #68

Not a whole day.

About the secret

A secret from the most ancient times. It means that when the knowledgeable, successful person perceives that action is required, he does not let even a whole day pass before taking the required action. Opportunity comes in a flash, and sometimes, disappears in a flash. When we see our opportunity before us, we should seize it and make it our own. In that way, we will not have to lament over lost opportunities, and our success will blossom like wildflowers in a sunny meadow after a spring rain.

Secret #69

*If we would rule,
we must first
learn to serve.*

About the secret

By first learning to serve, we will come to understand those who will eventually serve us. The only valid reason for a knowledgeable, successful person to want to rule is so he can better serve those whom he wishes to rule. If we are unprepared or unwilling to serve our followers, it is better for them, and for us, that we never achieve rulership because, if we do, and then cease to serve them, we will lose our following. All our efforts will have been for naught, and we will suffer great embarrassment. Only through serving can we obtain from those whom we rule the joyous assent that is necessary if they are to follow us.

Secret #70

*In friendships
and close relationships,
we must make a careful choice.*

About the secret

Certain people uplift us; others pull us down. Certain people give us strength; others drain our energy. We must choose carefully. Good friends, like good neighbors, are an endless benefit. Bad relationships can ruin a lifetime. Following the path of the knowledgeable, successful person permits a natural selection that will find us only with the best quality friends.

Secret #71

*If one clings
to the little boy,
one loses
the strong man.*

About the secret

At a point in our lives we must leave behind our childish ideas and our need to cling to someone else if we are to become strong, independent people. When we become parents, if we pamper our children, we will prevent them from becoming strong, independent adults. We cannot help our children beyond a certain point without precluding their gaining strength on their own. Sometimes a loving parent is the most difficult hurdle a developing child has to overcome. Similarly, at some point in our lives, we must leave behind all that binds us to our place, that holds us back: preconceived ideas, beliefs that do not benefit us, dependencies of every nature, and fear of the future. It takes courage, great courage, but here is a secret within a secret: we all have enough courage to overcome even our greatest fears. They come into the world together; fear and courage. We only need to call upon our courage to overcome even our worst fears.

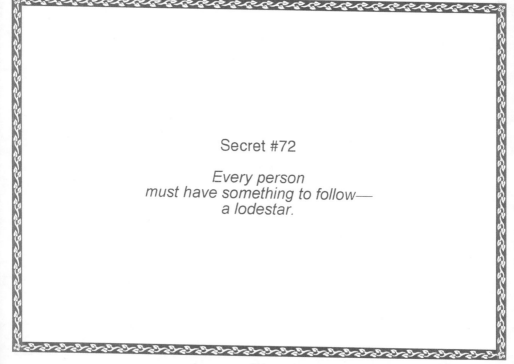

Secret #72

*Every person
must have something to follow—
a lodestar.*

About the secret

We all need something to bring out the best in ourselves and to provide direction for our development, such as the secrets in this book. By holding the image of the knowledgeable, successful person in our minds as our lodestar, and keeping aware of the secrets, we will achieve not only supreme success but also great happiness, peace and security.

Secret #73

*In following
the path of the knowledgeable, successful person,
slight digressions from the good
cannot be avoided,
but
we must turn back,
before going too far.*

About the secret

Having turned onto the path of the inferior person, and we all do that at times, it is only natural that we feel remorse, powerful remorse, but that is a good sign. However, we must not carry remorse too far; after making whatever amends are necessary, we must continue on, having resolved to be more cautious. To follow the path of the knowledgeable, successful person takes great courage, firm determination, and fierce perseverance. We must watch like hungry hawks for transgressions, and finding them, we must turn back. This is an act of self-mastery, and highly commendable. Having turned back, our progress will be like a hurricane, sweeping all obstacles from our path, and supreme good fortune and great success will quickly follow.

Secret #74

If
we are not as we should be
we will have misfortune,
and
it does not further us
to undertake
anything.

About the secret

The path of the inferior person is filled with pitfalls of his own making. In any plan or undertaking of which we conceive, there is always one constant: ourselves. If our characters are flawed, if we cannot depend upon ourselves to be efficient or careful or cautious or persevering or honorable, then we are a danger and a detriment to our own plans, and it does not profit us to undertake anything. If our character is without flaw, we can carry out even difficult and dangerous undertakings without fear of failure.

Secret #75

*Only
through daily self-renewal of character
can we continue
at the height of our powers.*

About the secret

It takes Herculean effort to reach the peak of perfection in any area of life and continuous effort to remain there. Every day some effort must be expended in refreshing ourselves with the ways of the knowledgeable, successful person. Reading great books, talking to like-minded people, teaching others, studying the deeds of our ancient heroes, thinking about our actions of the day to see whether we are being the best that we can be, all are ways to continue on the path. As we grow in awareness, our power will grow, and our attainments will be like the harvest after a perfect summer. There is no other activity that will reward us as richly as the daily self-renewing of our characters.

Secret #76

We have received a nature
that is innately good.
When our thoughts and actions
are in accord with our natures,
we will enjoy
great good fortune
and supreme success.

About the secret

It is true that we are divine incarnations, perfect beings. When, however, we act out of greed, selfishness, meanness, hatred, or other such inferior motives, we act the part of lesser beings and so experience pain, despair, and frustration. Those feelings are not a punishment, although they seem so, but only to let us know that we have departed from the path of the knowledgeable, successful person. Feelings of love and joy let us know that we are on the path. Whatever we are experiencing is a result of our intentions, our thoughts, and our actions. It is we who are in charge of our fate, and not another.

Secret #77

We should not set our eyes on the harvest
while planting it,
nor on the use of the ground
while clearing it.

About the secret

Every task must receive the attention it deserves if it is to turn out well. Anticipating the outcome of our efforts may cause us to become impatient and over-eager, hurrying to complete the task. Hasty or careless work will result in an unsatisfactory performance of the task, which, of course, will bring about an unsatisfactory result. We must do every task for its own sake, doing it as well as we can, and it can only happen that we will achieve good fortune and great success.

Secret #78

*Words are movements
going from within, outward.
Eating and drinking are movements
that go from without, inward.
Both movements can be modified by tranquillity.*

About the secret

Tranquillity is being calm and peaceful with a sense of well being. Everything, in its proper measure, benefits us. The same thing, carried to excess, destroys us. The way to achieve tranquillity is to follow the path of the knowledgeable, successful person who is careful of his words and temperate in eating and drinking. Always, it is the excesses, too much or too little, that destroy us. Moderation will always find us enjoying the great rewards of life.

Secret #79

*A situation only becomes favorable
when one adapts to it.*

About the secret

As long as we are angry, upset or feel hurt over an event or a situation, we will be unable to perceive its beneficial aspects, and we may wear ourselves out with unnecessary resistance; the event or situation may have been to our complete advantage from the first moment. Even happy turns of fortune sometimes come to us in a form that seems strange or unlucky. The event itself is simply an event and the situation is just the setting in which we find ourselves. The way we respond to the event or situation determines its final outcome in our lives. Once an event has taken place or a situation has been revealed to us, since we cannot alter the past, all that is left to us is our response. By responding as though what happened was completely for our benefit, we will immediately experience good feelings about what happened, and, by acting in accord with our feelings, we will naturally bring that about as a result of the Universal law of cause and effect. Those who know that one secret and act accordingly, will not only be masters of their fate, speeding quickly to the achievement of their goals, but will also enjoy a lifetime of heart warming happiness and abundant success.

Secret #80

*Danger
has an important
and beneficial
use.*

About the secret

Being aware of danger, causes us to take the necessary precautions that will protect us from harm when danger arises. By doing this we have used danger to further the achievement of our success and to protect what we already have.

Secret #81

Every ending contains a new beginning.

About the secret

The ending of one thing is always and instantly the beginning of another. The path of the knowledgeable, successful person, which only leads to supreme good fortune and great success, is always directly in front of us. We may take the first step upon it at any time and magically transform our circumstances. Because of the Universal law of cause and effect, these benefits are available to everyone, withheld from no one. The path of the inferior person is also always directly in front of us, bringing its lessons of hardship, misery and despair, but only so that we will ultimately come to know the truth. At each step of our way we must always choose between these two paths. Our futures are entirely in our own hands, and everything is possible.